Sports Illustrated KIDS

KNOW THE STATS

BASKETBALL
IS A NUMBERS GAME

by Eric Braun

CAPSTONE PRESS
a capstone imprint

Sports Illustrated Kids Know the Stats are published by Capstone Press,
a Capstone Imprint, 1710 Roe Crest Drive, North Mankato, Minnesota 56003.
www.mycapstone.com

Library of Congress Cataloging-in-Publication Data
is available on the Library of Congress website.
ISBN: 978-1-5435-0608-2 (library binding)
ISBN: 978-1-5435-0616-7 (eBook PDF)

Editorial Credits
Nate LeBoutillier, editor; Brent Slingsby, designer;
Eric Gohl, media researcher; Laura Manthe, production specialist

Photo Credits
Newscom: Cal Sport Media/Chris Szagola, 16, TNS/David Santiago, 8, USA Today Sports/Adam
Hunger, 24, USA Today Sports/Bill Streicher, 23, USA Today Sports/Brian Spurlock, 28, USA
Today Sports/Kyle Terada, 5, USA Today Sports/Troy Taormina, 13; Sports Illustrated: John G.
Zimmerman, 20, John W. McDonough, cover, 7, 10, 26, Robert Beck, 14, Simon Bruty, 18

Design Elements: Shutterstock

All statistics have been updated through the 2016–17 NBA season.

Printed in the United States of America.
010782S18

TABLE OF
CONTENTS

STATS & STORIES

Stories and Numbers

The Cleveland Cavaliers were down three games to none in the National Basketball Association (NBA) Finals on June 9, 2017. Their opponent, the Golden State Warriors, had breezed through the playoffs with 15 straight wins to that point. It looked like they'd win the Finals without losing a single game.

But Cleveland had other plans. That night, the Cavs were explosive right from the opening tip. They scored an NBA Finals record 49 points in the first quarter and had a record 86 by halftime. They also set a Finals record for 3-pointers with 24. LeBron James, the Cavs' brightest star, had 31 points, 11 assists, and 10 rebounds. It was his ninth career triple-double in the NBA Finals, which broke the record he'd shared with Magic Johnson. Cleveland won the game 137-116.

Of course, the end of the story is that Golden State bounced back to win Game 5 and claim the series. But for one night, the Cavs put up record-setting numbers against one of the most dominant champions in NBA history.

If you're a fan of basketball, there is nothing more exciting than watching a live NBA game. But even if you're not lucky enough to watch, the numbers can tell you a lot about how it went. Even when you do see a game, numbers are a fun way to relive it. Numbers tell stories.

Statistics help players, coaches, and executives too. Numbers help coaches figure out which players should play and which ones are best left on the bench. Numbers help executives understand which players are best at which skills and who to try to sign to the team. Analysts are constantly trying to improve statistics so they can tell us more — and help everyone to understand the game better.

LeBron James, forward, Cleveland Cavaliers

CHAPTER ONE

SHOOTING & SCORING

Individual Points Per Game (PPG)

Russell Westbrook and Kevin Durant were a dynamic duo. The Oklahoma Thunder teammates brought their team to the NBA Finals in 2012 when they were both just 23 years old. The future looked incredibly bright.

And then Durant decided to leave Oklahoma City after playing eight seasons with Westbrook. Before the 2017 season, he signed a free agent contract with the rival Golden State Warriors.

This naturally led to a falling out between Westbrook and Durant. Westbrook signed a long-term contract extension with OKC almost as if to prove Durant's disloyalty. And on the season's opening night he seemed more determined than ever, pouring in 32 points. The next night against Phoenix he scored 51. The night after that he notched 33. Then 35. Over the course of the season, Westbrook averaged 31.5 points per game (PPG), which led the league. This was an increase of 8.1 points per game from the previous season.

To get points per game, take total number of points divided by total number of games. In 2016–17, Westbrook scored 2,558 points in 81 games.

Points   Games

2,558   **81** $2{,}558 \div 81 = 31.6$

Keven Durant (left), small forward, and Russell Westbrook, point guard, as Oklahoma City Thunder teammates

Durant, meanwhile, saw his scoring number dip after joining a loaded Warriors team. The Warriors featured Stephen Curry, who averaged 30.1 PPG as the NBA's scoring leader in 2015–16. But the greatest players often sacrifice big points totals if it means greater success for their teams. So it was for both Warriors superstars. Durant averaged about three points fewer per game, and Curry averaged about five fewer.

How did it turn out in the end? Westbrook and Durant barely spoke during the 2016–17 season except for a couple of heated words on the court. Westbrook won the scoring title that year. But OKC was bounced in the first round of the playoffs. Meanwhile, the Warriors went on to win the title. And who was the NBA Finals Most Valuable Player (MVP) with an impressive 35.2 PPG in the championship series? Kevin Durant.

PPG Leaders, 2012–17

Season	Player	Team	PPG
2016-17	Russell Westbrook	Thunder	31.6
2015-16	Stephen Curry	Warriors	30.1
2014-15	Russell Westbrook	Thunder	28.1
2013-14	Kevin Durant	Thunder	32.0
2012-13	Carmelo Anthony	Knicks	28.7

3-Point Field Goals [3FG]

For an NBA-record 157 straight games, guard Stephen Curry of the Golden State Warriors made at least one 3-point shot. Then, in a game against the Los Angeles Lakers on November 4, 2016, he went cold. Very cold. Ten times against L.A., Curry hoisted a 3-pointer. Ten times he missed. Even worse, Curry's Warriors lost the game to the underdog Lakers.

Facing the New Orleans Pelicans three days later, the Warriors bounced back, and Curry got hot. Very hot. Curry caught fire from 3-point land by making 13 shots in 17 attempts. Curry's 13 treys set the single-game NBA record, and the Warriors won the game.

It's a good example of what makes Curry so fun to watch. Sure, he's a terrific ball handler. He has great court vision. But in the end, it comes down to one thing: The guy hits threes at an astonishing rate.

Stephen Curry, point guard, Golden State Warriors

Curry made 324 three-point baskets in the 2016–17 season. His teammate, Klay Thompson, made 268. They were first and second in the league.

Shooting threes is risky. They're harder to make. The league averaged 35.8 percent success on 3-pointers in 2016–17 compared to 45.7 percent on 2-pointers. With players like Curry and Thompson, the Warriors' risk is usually worth it because they make those tough shots at a higher rate than most players. Three-point percentage is calculated by dividing the total number of threes made by the number of threes attempted. Curry made his 324 threes off of 789 attempts in 2016–17. That means he made his threes 41.1 percent of the time.

3-Point Field Goals Made, 2016-17

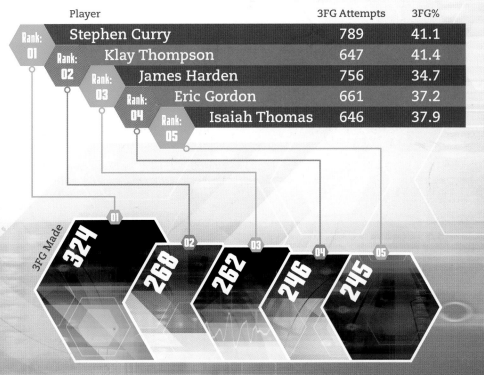

Rank	Player	3FG Attempts	3FG%
01	Stephen Curry	789	41.1
02	Klay Thompson	647	41.4
03	James Harden	756	34.7
04	Eric Gordon	661	37.2
05	Isaiah Thomas	646	37.9

3FG Made

01 324
02 268
03 262
04 246
05 245

DeAndre Jordan, center, Los Angeles Clippers

Field Goal Percentage (FG%)

When you *need* a bucket, who do you want taking that shot?

One way to answer that question is by looking at field goal percentage (FG%). That is the percentage of times a player's shots result in the ball going through the hoop — and points going on the board. If you take ten shots and make six of them, your field goal percentage rings up as 60. Players with a high FG% are more likely to sink their shots.

The 2016–17 leader in that category was DeAndre Jordan of the Los Angeles Clippers, who finished with a 71.4 FG%. That sky-high number was a whopping five percentage points higher than the next player on the list, Utah's Rudy Gobert, who shot 66.1 percent.

But Jordan scored only 12.7 PPG that year. There are two reasons for his low PPG. One is that he is a big man who scores all his points in the paint. He almost never shoots three-pointers. The other reason is that he struggles from the free-throw line. He made only 48.2 percent of his free throws in 2016–17. He even occasionally lofts airballs from the line.

Still, if your team is in need of a basket, it pays to get the ball to Jordan when he's close to the hoop. He'll probably make it. That is, if he doesn't get fouled. In that case, you may be in trouble.

FG% Leaders, 2016-17

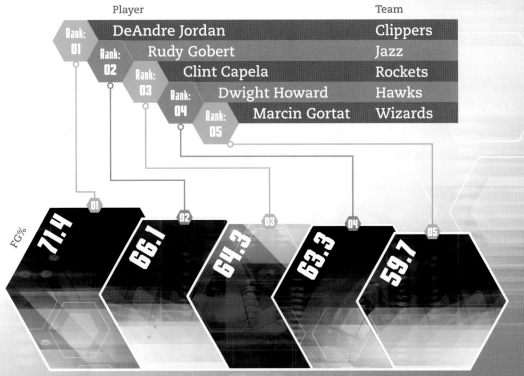

	Player	Team	FG%
Rank: 01	DeAndre Jordan	Clippers	71.4
Rank: 02	Rudy Gobert	Jazz	66.1
Rank: 03	Clint Capela	Rockets	64.3
Rank: 04	Dwight Howard	Hawks	63.3
Rank: 05	Marcin Gortat	Wizards	59.7

Effective Field Goal Percentage (eFG%)

Would you rather have a big man who shoots 64.3 FG%, or a wing player with a 51.6 FG%? If we only look at FG%, it appears the big man is a lot more valuable. But there's more to the story.

Let's take big man Clint Capela of the Houston Rockets for an example. Capela, a center, ranks among the league leaders in field goal percentage, but he didn't attempt a single three-pointer in 2016–17. Now let's take Washington Wizards small forward Otto Porter. His FG% may be lower, but he chips in a few threes. So some of those shots he's making are worth 50 percent more, point-wise, than Capela's shots.

Effective field goal percentage is a stat that takes the extra value of a three-pointer into account when analyzing a shooter's ability. Here's how it works: You take the player's total field goals and add one-half of his number of 3-pointers. Then you divide that number by the player's total attempts:

(*Field Goals* + **0.5** (*3-point Field Goals*)) ÷ ***Field Goal Attempts***

Porter made 414 field goals and 148 three-point shots out of a total 803 attempts.

FG	3FG x 0.5	FG Attempts
414	**74**	**803**

$$(414 + 74) \div 803 = .608$$

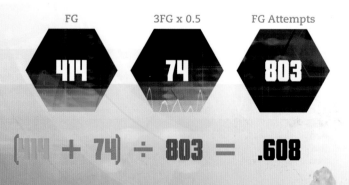

In comparison, Capela's eFG% was 64.3 percent (the same as his regular FG%). So he was still a more valuable shooter than Porter. But using eFG% showed that the value of these players was closer than it might first

eFG% Leaders, 2016–17

Rank	Player	eFG%
01	DeAndre Jordan	71.4
02	Rudy Gobert	66.1
03	Clint Capela	64.3
04	Dwight Howard	63.3
05	Otto Porter	60.8

Free Throw Percentage [FT%]

On January 29, 1989, Cleveland Cavaliers center Chris Dudley stepped up to the free throw line. He shot his two free throws and missed them both. This was nothing unusual. Dudley was a fair defender and rebounder. But free throw shooting? Not so much. That's when things got weird.

After Dudley's second miss, an opponent was called for a lane violation, so Dudley took a third shot. He missed that one too. But there was another lane violation on that shot. So Dudley was given yet another free throw. Which he missed. But the ref called a lane violation on that shot as well. Do we need to mention what happened with Dudley's fifth foul shot in a row? He clanked it, of course.

Some guys can make free throws in their sleep. Steve Nash, who played for the Phoenix Suns, Dallas Mavericks, and L.A. Lakers, retired with a career free throw percentage of 90.4, the best ever. Chris Dudley's career percentage was 45.8, which means Nash made free his throws at about twice the rate that Dudley did.

Steve Nash, point guard, Phoenix Suns

To calculate a player's free throw percentage, just divide the number of shots made by the number taken. Over his career, Nash shot 3,384 free throws and made 3,060 of them.

Shots Made: 3,060

Shots Taken: 3,384

$$3{,}060 \div 3{,}384 = .904$$

The free throw is a simple shot. It's not as exciting as a long three or a dunk. The clock's not even running. But free throws are critical to winning games. Just ask Chris Dudley, whose Cavaliers lost that 1989 game . . . by five points.

Career FT% Leaders

Rank	Player	Teams
01	Steve Nash	Suns, Mavericks, Lakers
02	Mark Price	Cavs, Magic, Bullets, Warriors
03	Stephen Curry*	Warriors
04	Peja Stojakovic	Kings, 4 other teams
05	Chauncey Billups	Pistons, 6 other teams

*active player

FT%

01: 90.4
02: 90.3
03: 90.1
04: 89.5
05: 89.4

CHAPTER TWO

DEFENSE & REBOUNDING

Blocks [BLK]

On April 12, 2017, after losing center Andrew Bogut to injury, the Cavaliers signed little-known center Edy Taveras. He played only one game for Cleveland, but in that game he blocked a ridiculous six shots.

Rudy Gobert, center, Utah Jazz

Taveras was inactive for the postseason, but his debut gave Cleveland fans a jolt and made them notice him. A colossal presence rejecting shots in the paint can be a real difference maker for any team, even one with LeBron James on it.

Seven-foot-one Frenchman Rudy Gobert of the Utah Jazz led the league in 2016–17 with 2.6 blocked shots per game. The NBA's 2016–17 Defensive Player of the Year runner-up was nicknamed "The Stifle Tower" for his sturdy defense. The Jazz made a valiant playoff run in the 2017 playoffs thanks in part to Gobert's rim protection. With his defensive prowess, hoops fans in Utah will enjoy a competitive team for years to come.

In 2016–17 Gobert blocked 214 shots in 81 games.

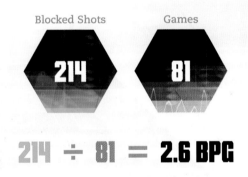

Blocked Shots: 214 Games: 81

214 ÷ 81 = 2.6 BPG

Most Blocked Shots Per Game, 2016-17

Rank	Player	Team	BPG
01	Rudy Gobert	Jazz	2.6
02	Anthony Davis	Pelicans	2.2
03	Myles Turner	Pacers	2.1
04	Hassan Whiteside	Heat	2.1
05	Kristaps Porzingis	Knicks	2.0

John Wall, point guard, Washington Wizards

Steals [STL]

After the Washington Wizards failed to make the playoffs in 2016, coach Scott Brooks challenged his point guard, John Wall, to get better. Wall was already a star, but he wasn't considered one of the greats. Missing the postseason hurt Wall more than his two knees he'd injured that year.

Wall accepted the challenge and played the 2016–17 season with increased intensity and aggression. The results can be seen in his stats, which were the best of his career. He averaged 23.1 points and 10.7 assists per game. His previous highs had been 19.9 points and 10.2 assists. He even bested his already-excellent rate of steals. He ripped off 157 steals that year — an average of 2.0 per game, which was the best in the league.

Career Steals

Rank	Player	Teams	Years
01	John Stockton	Jazz	1984–2003
02	Jason Kidd	Mavericks, Suns, Nets, Knicks	1994–2013
03	Michael Jordan	Bulls, Wizards	1984–2003
04	Gary Payton	SuperSonics, 4 other teams	1990–2007
05	Maurice Cheeks	76ers, 4 other teams	1978–93

Steals

01 **3,265**
02 **2,684**
03 **2,514**
04 **2,445**
05 **2,310**

Like blocks, steals put a quick end to an opponent's attack. Steals can be exciting and fun. They often lead to the game's most exciting moments, which usually occur on fast breaks. A great fast break charges up fans and players alike.

But stealing is a gambler's game. Trying for a steal and missing usually results with the defender out of position. He can't defend his man, who suddenly has an open shot or lane to the basket. Most of the time, it's best to play straight-up D. That is, unless you're an elite ball thief like Wall or Golden State's Draymond Green.

John Stockton is the all-time leading ball thief. During his 20-year NBA career, he filched a whopping 3,265 steals. That's 581 more than the runner-up on the list, Jason Kidd.

Whether it's a slam-dunk, a layup, or a fade-away jumper, a successful basket means points on the board. But what happens when a shot doesn't go in? Someone needs to grab the rebound.

Offensive rebounds keep possessions alive and can crush even the best of defenses. Defensive boards can be as valuable as turnovers.

Hall of Famer Bill Russell won 11 championships with the Boston Celtics in the 1960s. He was a five-time MVP, but he never finished higher than 15th in the league in scoring. One of the things that made him so valuable was his rebounding. Russell pulled down 21,620 rebounds in his career — including 53 in one game.

Bill Russell, center, Boston Celtics

Wilt Chamberlain holds many NBA records. He led the league in rebounding 11 times, and he still holds the career record for rebounds per game (RPG) at **22.9**.

You can figure out a player's rebounds per game by dividing his total number of rebounds by the number of games played. Chamberlain pulled down 23,924 rebounds in his career and played 1,045 games.

Rebounds 23,924 Games 1,045

23,924 ÷ 1,045 = 22.9 REBOUNDS PER GAME

In today's NBA, Dwight Howard is among the best in the business. His rate of 12.7 RPG in 2016–17 was right in line with his career average of 12.7. That's good for 13th on the all-time list.

Rebounds Per Game, Career

Rank	Player	Teams	Years	TRB
01	Wilt Chamberlain	Warriors, 76ers, Lakers	1959–73	22.9
02	Bill Russell	Celtics	1956–69	22.5
03	Bob Pettit	Hawks	1954–65	16.2
04	Jerry Lucas	Royals, Warriors, Knicks	1963–74	15.6
05	Nate Thurmond	Warriors, Bulls, Cavs	1963–77	15.0

CHAPTER THREE

ALL-AROUND VALUE

Real Plus/Minus [RPM]

Robert Covington didn't get drafted in 2013. He signed onto Houston's developmental league team and won defensive rookie of the year.

Covington didn't always look good on the court. His shooting was streaky. His bad days were really bad. But he eventually got his NBA shot with the Philadelphia 76ers. The team just seemed to play better when he was on the court. He was not a superstar. But he played an important role on the team — even if traditional statistics didn't show it. However, there is a stat that shows his value. It's called Real Plus/Minus (RPM).

2016-17 RPM Leaders

Rank	Player	Team	RPM
01	LeBron James	Cavaliers	8.42
02	Chris Paul	Clippers	7.92
03	Stephen Curry	Warriors	7.41
04	Draymond Green	Warriors	7.14
05	Kawhi Leondard	Spurs	7.08

The original plus/minus stat looks at a team's point differential when a player is on the floor compared with when he's not. It measures what happens overall when a player is on the court. But there's a problem with plus/minus. It can be heavily affected by other players on the court. If an average player gets to play with superstar teammates all the time, he'll look pretty good.

That's where RPM comes in. The formula is complicated, but it analyzes 230,000 possessions each NBA season. Then it measures each player's impact and adjusts for the effect of his teammates and opponents. RPM estimates how many points each player adds or subtracts, on average, to his team's net scoring. Then it scales the scoring for each 100 possessions played, which is about the length of one game.

So how did Covington compare to other players in 2016–17? His RPM was +3.55, tops on his team. He was the 25th most valuable player in the league by that measure.

Robert Covington, small forward, Philadelphia 76ers

Triple-Doubles

How do you measure all-around dominance in basketball? Is it by scoring the most points? Scoring is only one part of the game.

One of the best measures of offensive dominance is the triple-double. That's when a player gets double digits in three categories — usually points, rebounds, and assists — in a single game. To get a triple-double, a player must be able to multitask and hustle all game long.

Russell Westbrook pulled off an amazing statistical feat in 2016–17 when he averaged a triple-double over the course of an entire season. On the year, Westbrook averaged 31.6 points, 10.7 rebounds, and 10.4 assists per game. He registered 42 triple-doubles during the season to break the previous season record of 41 held by Oscar Robertson.

Russell Westbrook, point guard, Oklahoma City Thunder

Robertson, who played for Cincinnati and Milwaukee back in the 1960s and 1970s, is the NBA's career leader in triple-doubles. The Hall of Famer and 12-time All-Star did it 181 times.

The 2016–17 season was quite the year for triple-doubles. The Rockets' James Harden hung 22 triple-doubles on the board, which was second in the NBA, and LeBron James was third with 13. Speaking of LeBron, he put up his ninth triple-double in an NBA Finals game. That is a record. His Finals record topped the mark previously held by legendary Lakers point guard Magic Johnson.

Most Career Triple-Doubles

Rank	Player	Teams	Years
01	Oscar Robertson	Royals, Bucks	1960–74
02	Magic Johnson	Lakers	1979–96
03	Jason Kidd	Mavericks, Suns, Nets, Knicks	1994–2013
04	Russell Westbrook	Thunder	2008–17*
05	Wilt Chamberlain	Warriors, 76ers, Lakers	1956–73

*active player

Triple-Doubles

01 — 181
02 — 138
03 — 107
04 — 79
05 — 78

James Harden, point guard, Houston Rockets

Assists Per Turnover [AST/TO]

April 12, 2017. Houston Rockets and Minnesota Timberwolves. The last regular-season game of the year. The playoffs are already set. This game is meaningless. Until it isn't.

Rockets point guard James Harden gets a screen and drives left. A defender picks him up. Harden could go for the shot, but instead he bounces a nearly invisible pass to teammate Nene. Nene receives the ball as easily as if it was handed to him on a pillow, and then he slams it home. Two points.

It was just one basket in an unimportant game. But here's why it was important: It was Harden's jaw-dropping 900th assist of the season. An assist is when a player completes a pass to a teammate that leads directly to a field goal, and Harden finished the season with 907 of them. That was the 25th highest single-season total of all time (and 67 more than the second player that season, Russell Westbrook). Harden averaged 11.2 assists per game.

Assists are a great measure of ball handling ability, but they're not the only one. So are turnovers, for the opposite reason. Turnovers are when a player loses possession of the ball to an opponent before his team takes a shot.

Consider Clippers point guard Chris Paul. He averaged fewer assists than Harden — a still-impressive 9.2 — but he turned it over only 2.4 times per game. In comparison, Harden averaged 5.7 turnovers.

Harden undoubtedly had one of the greatest offensive seasons in NBA history. But by looking at his ratio of assists-to-turnovers, we see that he turned the ball over half as often as he got an assist. On the other hand, Paul's ratio was much lower. He looks like the superior ball handler. Fans in Houston can compare the two easily as Paul signed on to play with Harden and the Rockets for the 2017–18 season.

Assists Per Turnover Leaders, 2016-17

Rank	Player	Team	Assists	Turnovers	AST/TO
01	Chris Paul	Clippers	563	147	3.83
02	Ish Smith	Pistons	418	112	3.73
03	Ricky Rubio	Timberwolves	682	195	3.50
04	T.J. McConnell	76ers	534	159	3.36
05	Tim Frazier	Pelicans	335	101	3.32

Player Efficiency Rating [PER]

Most stats tell us one particular detail about a player's (or a team's) performance. By looking at a combination of stats, we can start to see a bigger picture emerge. But sometimes it's helpful to look at one statistic that tries to measure the big picture all on its own. That's what player efficiency rating (PER) does.

Developed by a sportswriter named John Hollinger, PER rates a player's overall productivity. It takes all of the player's positive feats such as field goals, free throws, 3-pointers, assists, rebounds, blocks, and steals. Then it looks at all the negative ones, like missed shots, turnovers, and personal fouls. It gives each of these actions a value, plugs them into a complicated formula, and spits out a single number. That number tells you how efficient a player is per minute.

League average PER is always 15.00. Everyone starts there. If a player's PER is higher than 15.00, he is an above average player. If his PER is lower, he's below average.

Kawhi Leonard, forward, San Antonio Spurs

PER also shows which players are on the rise so fans can predict who might be the biggest stars of tomorrow's NBA. Kawhi Leonard's stellar 27.6 PER in 2016–17 was third in the league. But he didn't come out of nowhere. He was sixth best the year before that, and 13th on the list back in 2014–15.

Karl-Anthony Towns of the Minnesota Timberwolves had the 13th best PER in his rookie year (2015–16). The next year he hit number 11 on the list with a 25.9. As one of the game's bright young stars, he's sure to improve his PER even more as he improves his game.

PER Leaders 2016-17

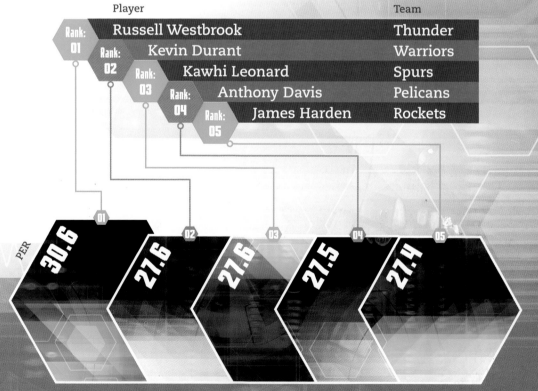

	Player	Team
Rank: 01	Russell Westbrook	Thunder
Rank: 02	Kevin Durant	Warriors
Rank: 03	Kawhi Leonard	Spurs
Rank: 04	Anthony Davis	Pelicans
Rank: 05	James Harden	Rockets

PER

01 — 30.6
02 — 27.6
03 — 27.6
04 — 27.5
05 — 27.4

GLOSSARY

airball — when a shot misses so badly it doesn't even touch the rim

assist — a pass that leads directly to a field goal score

ball handling — control of the ball by skillful dribbling and passing

fast break — a play where a team takes control of the ball and moves down the court quickly to try to score before the defense gets into position

lane violation — a violation called when a player steps into the lane before a free-throw shooter releases the ball

paint — the free throw lane or square painted area on a basketball court

possession — the time a team has offensive possesion of the basketball until it scores, loses the ball, or commits a rule violation

post — the name for a player or area on the court that is located very near the basket

rebound — gaining hold of a ball that bounces off the rim or backboard following a shot attempt

screen — a blocking move by an offensive player to free up a teammate to shoot, receive a pass, or drive toward the rim; also known as a pick

triple-double — performance in which a player reaches double-digit totals in three offensive categories, usually points, rebounds, and assists

turnover — occurs when a team loses possession of the ball to the opponent before getting a chance to attempt a shot

wing — the name for a player or area on the court that is located to the side of the court, out away from the basket

READ MORE

Editors of Sports Illustrated. *Sports Illustrated Basketball's Greatest.* New york: Sports Illustrated, 2014.

Chandler, Matt. *The Science of Basketball.: The Top Ten Ways Science Affects the Game.* Top 10 Science. North Mankato, Minn.: Capstone Press, 2016.

Braun, Eric. *TPro Basketball's Underdogs: Players and Teams Who Shocked the Basketball World.* North Mankato, Minn.: Capstone Press, 2018.

INTERNET SITES

Use FactHound to find internet sites related to this book.

Visit www.facthound.com

Just type in 9781543506082 and go.

 Check out projects, games and lots more at **www.capstonekids.com**

INDEX